Mortimer the Moose and the Alphabet Zoo

Mortimer and Rolando

Mortimer the Moose and the Alphabet Zoo

By Joe Broadmeadow

and

Levi David Walkup, Special Adviser to the Author

Mortimer and Rolando Illustrations by Kendra Beauregard

Animal Illustrations Shutterstock

Copyright

Copyright © 2022 by JEBWizard Publishing
All rights reserved.
This book or any portion thereof may not be reproduced or used in any manner whatsoever without the publisher's express written permission, except for the use of brief quotations in a book review.
Printed in the United States of America by IngramSpark
10 9 8 7 6 5 4 3 2 1 24 23 22 21
First Printing, 2022
ISBN
Hardcover 979-8-9850177-3-1
Paperback 979-8-9850177-5-5
ePub 979-8-9850177-4-8
JEBWizard Publishing
37 Park Forest Rd.
Cranston, RI 02920
www.jebwizardpublishing.com

JEBWizard Publishing
Books with Character

Dedication

This book is dedicated to all who instilled in me a love of reading— and the desire to pass it on to others— all those years ago.

Reading, especially the most precious act of reading to others, is the best foundation for a happy and fulfilled life.

Enjoy!

Joe Broadmeadow and Levi David Walkup

The Real Mortimer and Rolando

Joe Broadmeadow and Levi David Walkup

What's an Alphabet?

One day, Mortimer the Moose, and his friend, Rolando the Racoon, were playing in the backyard.

"Hey Rolando, what's an alphabet?"

"I don't know," said Rolando. "Why are you asking me?"

"Well, I heard our friend Levi will have to learn the alphabet someday and I want to help him."

"Hmm," said Rolando, "hmm, hmm, hmm," tapping his tail on the ground. Then a huge smile crossed his face. "I know. Let's go ask the animals in the zoo. One of them is bound to know what an alphabet is."

"Good idea, Rolando, let's go."

So the two friends walked down the sidewalk, checking both ways before crossing the street, waving to all the cars beeping at them, and made it to the zoo.

"Where do we start?" asked Mortimer

"It's always best to start at the beginning," said Rolando. "So let's just go to the first animal we see and work our way around the whole place."

Up ahead was a sign,

Arnie the Aardvark.

Joe Broadmeadow and Levi David Walkup

(A) Arnie the Aardvark

Mortimer leaned over the fence. "Excuse me, Mr. Aardvark. Do you know what an alphabet is?"

"I most certainly do not. I know what different ants taste like and how to find them, but I've never eaten an alphabet and have no idea what that is."

"Thank you, anyway," said Mortimer, and they moved on.

The next sign read,

Bernie the Baboon

Joe Broadmeadow and Levi David Walkup

(B)Bernie the Baboon

Mortimer looked up at the baboon swinging in the branches. "Excuse me, Mr. Baboon. Do you know what an alphabet is?"

"Alphabet? *ALPHABET?* I have no need for an alphabet, whatever that is. I have my branches to swing on and my fruit to eat.

"You and that funny-looking cat need to go away."

"Hey, you," Rolando said. "I'm not a cat, I'm a raccoon. We're smarter than any old cat."

"Hoo, hoo, hoo, whaaahh waaahh" screamed the Baboon. So Mortimer and Rolando moved on.

The next sign read,

Chuck the Cheetah.

Joe Broadmeadow and Levi David Walkup

(C) Chuck the Cheetah

The cheetah, crouched down, kept an eye on Mortimer and Rolando as they came closer.

His muscles twitched, and he licked his snout.

"Excuse me, Mr. Cheetah. Do you know what an alphabet is?"

"I might," Cheetah smiled, "but it's hard to think when I'm hungry. Toss me that raccoon and I might be able to help you."

Mortimer glanced at Rolando, then back at the Cheetah.

"Hey, you're not thinking of throwing me in there, are you?" Rolando backed away.

"Of course not, you're my friend." Mortimer laughed. "Let's just keep going."

The next sign said,

Donald the Deer

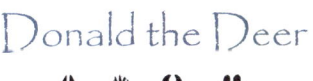

Joe Broadmeadow and Levi David Walkup

(D)Donald the Deer

At the deer enclosure, the herd was browsing for acorns. Donald the Deer walked over to the fence.

"Hey there cousin Moose, what can I do for you?"

"Excuse me, Mr. Deer. Do you know what an alphabet is?"

"Why so formal? Call me Donald. But an alphabet, hmm. Sounds familiar but I'm not really sure." He turned to look at all the other deer.

"Hey, anybody here know what an alphabet is?"

Every deer looked up but continued to chew. Then, one by one, went back to grazing.

"Sorry, cousin, can't help you." Donald wandered back to the herd.

The next sign said,

Evangeline the Ermine

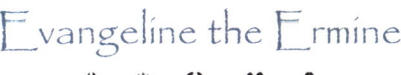

Joe Broadmeadow and Levi David Walkup

(E)Evangeline the Ermine

Mortimer and Rolando walked to the next enclosure. "Maybe you should try to ask this time, Rolando."

"Okay," Rolando shrugged. "I will use my charming personality.

"Hey Ermine, what's an alphabet?"

Evangeline swished her white tail, ignoring Rolando. Licking her paws, she pretended like she had heard nothing.

"Be polite, Rolando, be polite," said Mortimer.

Rolando frowned but tried his best. "Excuse me, Ms. Evangeline, might you know what an alphabet is?"

The Ermine smiled. "That's better Mr. Raccoon. While I do not *know* what an alphabet is, I know it needs letters. I saw the caretaker using something called letters when he made my new sign."

"Thank you, Evangeline. We will move on," said Rolando.

"See, Rolando, being polite always works."

The next sign read,

Frankie the Frog.

Joe Broadmeadow and Levi David Walkup

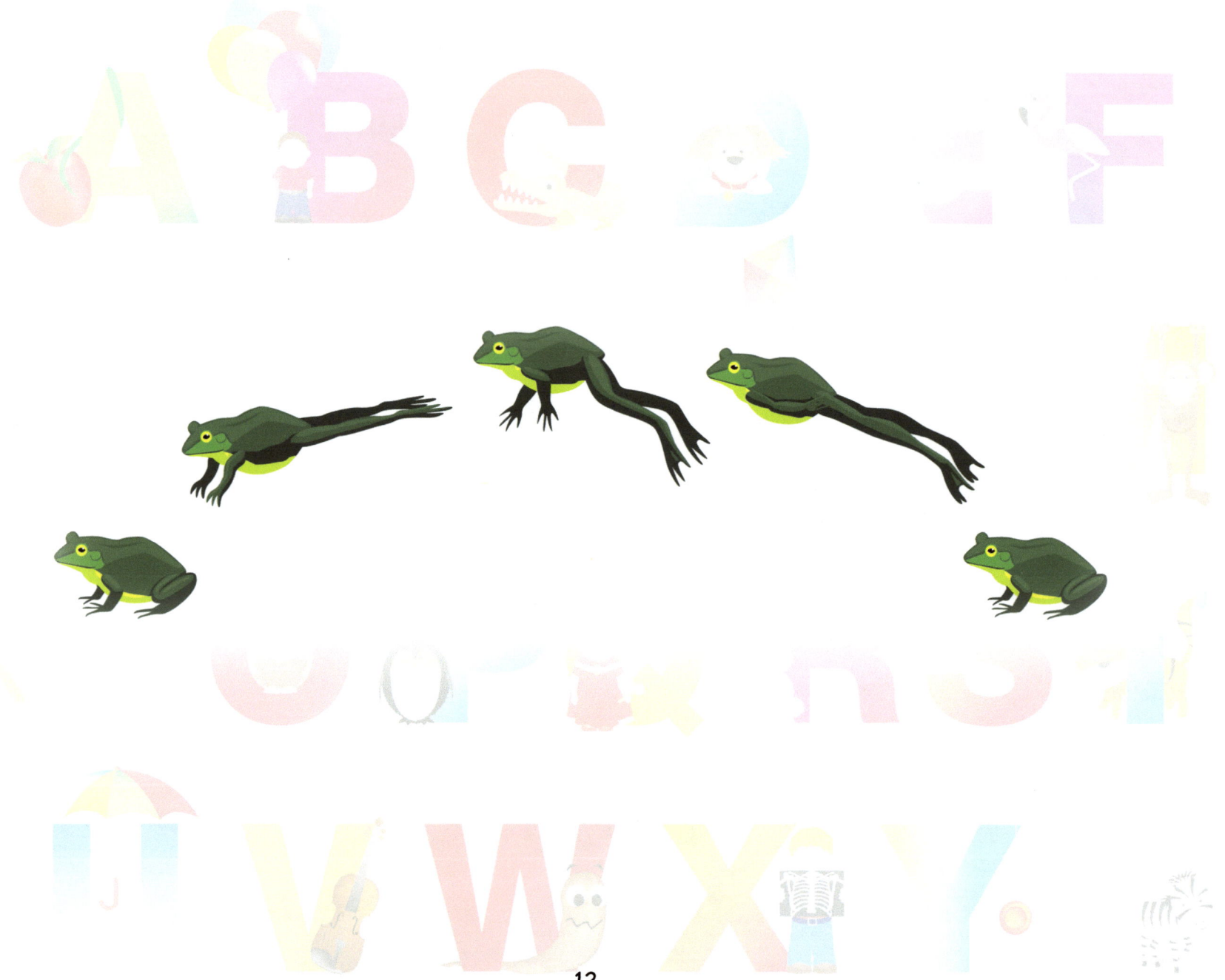

(F)Frankie the Frog

Frankie the frog sat on a stump hanging over a green, scum-covered pond, his eyes darting back and forth, looking for fat, juicy flies.

"Hello, Frankie," said Mortimer, "can I ask you a question?"

Frankie looked at Mortimer, started to speak, then jumped away. His tongue slashed out, snagged a fly, and then disappeared back into Frankie's mouth.

"Ewww," said Rolando, "he's eating a fly."

"Of course he is," said Mortimer, "it's what frogs eat."

"That's gross," said Rolando, his face scrunched up, cringing at the thought.

Mortimer waited for Frankie to finish his lunch (he knew he was done when Frankie let out a tremendous rrrrriiiibbbbbiiiittt, which is a frog burb!)

"Frankie, do you know what an alphabet is?"

"Hmm," said Frankie, "hmm, hmm, hmm. I don't think I do. But that know-it-all giraffe next door is always looking around. He might."

"Thank you," said Mortimer, "I hope you catch more flies."

The next sign read,

Joe Broadmeadow and Levi David Walkup

Joe Broadmeadow and Levi David Walkup

(G)George the Giraffe

George the Giraffe stood tall, very tall, eating leaves from the tippety-top of a tree.

Mortimer looked at Rolando. "I'm not sure he'll hear us way up there."

"Just yell," said Rolando. "Use your outside moose voice."

Mortimer took a deep breath then yelled as loud as he could. "GEORGE THE GIRAFFE CAN WE ASK YOU A QUESTION?"

George looked down, still chewing leaves, then bent his long, long neck down to face Mortimer.

"Mr. Moose, I am not deaf, you know, just tall. There is no need to yell."

Mortimer shrugged. "Sorry, but do you know what an alphabet is?"

"An alphabet, why an alphabet is, ahh, you see, ahh. I can't explain it but of course I know what it is." He blinked twice, then stretched his neck back up to the treetops.

Mortimer looked at Rolando. "He doesn't know, does he?"

"Nope," said Rolando. "Next."

The next sign read,

Joe Broadmeadow and Levi David Walkup

Joe Broadmeadow and Levi David Walkup

(H)Harry the Hippopotamus

When Mortimer and Rolando got to the edge of the Hippo pond, all they could see were bubbles in the water.

"Where's the Hippo?" asked Rolando. "They're pretty big, aren't they?"

"Wait for it," said Mortimer.

And with that, an enormous set of eyes popped up out of the water, followed by a humongous head. Then the Hippo opened his gigantic mouth.,

"He wants to swallow us," yelled Rolando, hiding behind Mortimer.

"No he doesn't," Mortimer said. "Hippos eat plants, not raccoons or moose." He turned to the Hippo. "Excuse me, Harry, do you know what an alphabet is?"

The Hippo said nothing, just shook his enormous head, spraying water all over Mortimer and Rolando, then sunk back under the water.

"Thanks, I think," said Mortimer, shaking his antlers to dry off.

The next sign read,

"

(I)na the Iguana

Rolando and Mortimer stood next to the iguana's home.

"How may I help you?" said a voice.

"Who said that?" asked Rolando, looking around but seeing nothing.

"I did," said Ina the Iguana, changing from the green of the trees to a soft brown and stepping slowly, each step a series of short hesitant motions, until she stood in front of Mortimer and Rolando.

"How does she do that?" asked Rolando.

"Iguana magic," said Mortimer, turning back to face the iguana. "Ina, do you know what an alphabet is?"

Ina climbed back up the tree. As she did, her colors would change to match the background. "I have heard of such things, this alphabet. But I am not sure what it is."

"Thanks, anyway," Mortimer said as Ina faded away.

"That's scary," said Rolando.

"Not if you're an Iguana," said Mortimer and headed back to the path.

The next sign read,

Joe Broadmeadow and Levi David Walkup

(J) Joey the Jackal

"I'm not sure I want to talk to this guy," Rolando said.

"Why not?" asked Mortimer.

"Jackals are scary and I bet they eat raccoons."

"No they don't. The animals here are well fed by the people who care for them. Stop worrying." Mortimer approached the edge of the enclosure. The jackal stood still, eyeing the two with beady little eyes.

"Is he drooling?" asked Rolando. "I think he's drooling."

"No, he's not," said Mortimer, glancing at the Jackal. "But just in case, stay back a ways." Mortimer moved in front of Rolando. "Excuse me, Mr. Jackal, do you know what an alphabet is?"

The jackal stared back at Mortimer, occasionally licking his lips. "I'm a bit hungry at the moment and can't think. Perhaps if I ate someone, er something, I might be able to help." A long drool fell to the ground as the Jackal eyed Rolando.

"Never mind," said Mortimer, "never mind. Come on, Rolando."

The next sign said,

Joe Broadmeadow and Levi David Walkup

Joe Broadmeadow and Levi David Walkup

(K)Kelsey the Kangaroo

Kelsey the Kangaroo bounced all around the field where she lived, racing past as Mortimer and Rolando stood watching her.

"I don't think she wants to talk," said Rolando.

"Sure she does," said Mortimer. "Just be patient."

A few moments later, Kelsey came bounding over and stood right in front of them.

"Hi there, Kelsey," said Mortimer.

"Shhhh," said Kelsey, "I'm trying to get the little one to sleep."

"Little one? What little one?" said Rolando.

Kelsey pointed to her pouch and Rolando and Mortimer could see a tiny sleeping baby kangaroo.

"Oh, sorry," whispered Mortimer. "We're trying to find out what an alphabet is."

"Sorry," Kelsey shrugged. "I'm so busy taking care of little Joey here I have no time to help." With that, she bounded off once again.

"How does he sleep in that pouch getting bounced everywhere?" asked Rolando

"I don't know," said Mortimer, "I'm not a kangaroo."

The next sign said,

Joe Broadmeadow and Levi David Walkup

(L)Lewis the Lion

Lewis the Lion lay in the sun, his tail swishing back and forth. He didn't move at all while he watched Mortimer and Rolando walk to his enclosure.

"Good day, Lewis," said Mortimer. "Might we have a word?"

The lion stretched his long legs, flexed his claws, and let out a yawn. "Mortimer, my friend, it has been a long time since you've come to see me."

"You know a lion?" asked Rolando.

"We met a long time ago, Rolando. Lewis and I are old friends."

"It's good to have a lion for a friend," said Rolando.

The lion rose to his feet and walked over to stand at the edge of his home. "What can I do for you, my friend?"

"Do you know what an alphabet is?" asked Mortimer

"Hmm, can't say as I do. I usually spend my time lounging in the sun and never had a need for an alphabet, whatever that is. Sorry, can't help you."

"Thanks anyway, Lewis," said Mortimer.

With that, Lewis lolled back to his sunny spot, rolled onto his back, and promptly fell asleep.

The next sign said,

Joe Broadmeadow and Levi David Walkup

(M) Marty the Mouse

"So where's the mouse?" asked Rolando.

"Watch this," said Mortimer, and tossed a few breadcrumbs onto the ground.

"I don't see anything," said Rolando.

"Be patient, Rolando, be patient."

Soon, twitching whiskers surrounding a tiny black nose poked up out of a small hole, then a mouse slowly popped out, ran over, grabbed the breadcrumbs, then started back toward his hole.

"Excuse me, Marty, could we ask you a question?" said Mortimer.

Marty glanced around, munching the breadcrumbs. "Okay, but be quick, I don't like being out in the open like this."

"Do you know what an alphabet is?"

"Nope, but I know it has something to do with letters. Of course, I don't know what a letter is, but that's what I heard. We mice hear a lot from our hiding places."

"Thanks anyway, Marty," Mortimer said, tossing him so more breadcrumbs.

The next sign said,

Joe Broadmeadow and Levi David Walkup

(N) Nina the Nightingale

Mortimer and Rolando wandered along the path, listening to the magical singing of the nightingale.

"The nightingale sings such a beautiful song, doesn't she?" said Mortimer.

"Beautiful," said Rolando. "Let's just rest and listen a moment."

After a few moments, the two walked to the enclosure where the nightingale sat on a branch singing away.

"Ms. Nightingale, that is a beautiful song you're singing. But could you answer a question?"

The nightingale stopped signing for a moment and nodded.

"Do know what an alphabet is?"

The nightingale shook her head no, then started singing again.

"Wow, a bird of few words, I suppose," said Rolando

"Yup" said Mortimer

The next sign said,

Joe Broadmeadow and Levi David Walkup

(O) Oscar the Ocelot

"Mortimer, what is an ocelot?" asked Rolando

"Kind of an oversized cat with an attitude," said Mortimer, "and they are beautiful, aren't they?" Mortimer pointed to the Ocelot grooming his paws. "Excuse us, Mr. Ocelot, but might you know what an alphabet is?"

The ocelot stopped what he was doing, stretched one leg, then the other, then all his legs, licked the fur on his chest, then walked over to stand near Mortimer.

"Here's what I know. An alphabet has twenty-six things called letters. As to what a letter is, that I cannot help you." The ocelot turned away, swishing his tail back and forth as he wandered back to a spot in the sun and resumed grooming himself.

The next sign said,

Joe Broadmeadow and Levi David Walkup

Joe Broadmeadow and Levi David Walkup

(P)Pam the Panda

Pam the Panda lay upside down on a branch munching on some bamboo shoots. Chewing slowly, she watched as Mortimer and Rolando looked up at her.

"How are we going to ask her anything if she's way up there?" asked Rolando.

"Be patient," said Mortimer, "she'll come down soon enough."

With that, Pam pulled herself upright and made her way down the tree trunk, still chewing on the bamboo.

"Hi, Mortimer," she said. "I hear you want to know about an alphabet."

Mortimer glanced at Rolando. "Whey, yes we do. How did you know?"

"I hear much while making my way through the trees. I wish I could be more helpful, but all I know is an alphabet has letters and letters can make words. But I have no idea what a word is." With that she made her way back up the tree, grabbed a fresh bamboo shoot, and munched happily away.

"See, Rolando," said Mortimer, "with everyone we ask, we learn a little more. Now we have to find out what words are."

The next sign said,

Joe Broadmeadow and Levi David Walkup

Joe Broadmeadow and Levi David Walkup

(Q) Quentin the Quail

"What kind of a name is Quentin?" asked Rolando.

"It's a bit different, but I like it," said Mortimer. "And you may be on to something, my friend."

Rolando stopped and looked at Mortimer. "How's that?"

"Well, we've been asking all our friends here what an alphabet is, but how is it we know their names?"

"Duh!" said Rolando, "because there are signs with the names."

"And how do we know what the sign says?"

"Because we read them."

"Exactly," said Mortimer, waving at Quentin the Quail. "We've been asking the wrong question." He turned to look at the Quail. "Quentin, who put up the sign with your name on it?"

"I'm not sure. It was here when I got here. But Rhonda might know," bobbing his head toward the next enclosure.

This next sign said,

Rhonda the Rabbit

Joe Broadmeadow and Levi David Walkup

(R)Rhonda the Rabbit

Rhonda the Rabbit sat munching grass, glancing around as she ate. Mortimer and Rolando stopped for a moment at her sign, then walked over to talk to her.

"Hi, Rolando. Hi Mortimer," Rhonda said. "Would you like some fresh grass?"

"No thank you," said Mortimer, "but I have a question for you."

Rhonda stopped chewing and hopped over to the fence. "Ask away, my friend."

"Who put up your sign?" asked Mortimer.

"Oh, that was Allison and Bert. They take care of us every day."

"Do you know where we can find them?"

"They were just here a few minutes ago. I'm sure they went to see Sally next," said Rhonda.

"Thanks, Rhonda. Enjoy your lunch. Come on, Rolando, let's try to catch up to Allison and Bert."

The next sign said,

Sally the Snake

Joe Broadmeadow and Levi David Walkup

(S) Sally the Snake

"Do we really have to talk to the snake?" asked Rolando. "They scare me."

"Why?" asked Mortimer. "Snakes are just misunderstood. They are actually quite friendly if you are friendly to them."

"Yeah, well, you talk to her. I'll stay right behind you just in case."

"In case what? You need to run away." Mortimer laughed.

Sally slithered over to see what was going on. "Rolando, come on over and let me give you a hug."

Rolando peeked out from behind Mortimer. "No thanks. Just tell us if you've seen Allison and Bert."

Sally coiled herself around a tree stump, then turned her head toward the next path. "They were going to work on Tommy the Turtle's sign. It needed some new letters.

"Great!" said Mortimer. "Did you hear that, Rolando? They are painting letters. Thanks, Sally. Come on Rolando, let's hurry so we can catch up to them."

They headed toward the next sign that said,

Tommy the Turtle

Joe Broadmeadow and Levi David Walkup

(T) Tommy the Turtle

Mortimer and Rolando raced down the path. As they passed the sign, they saw a notice that said, WET PAINT!

"They must have just been here. Let's hurry," said Mortimer. They rushed over to the turtle enclosure. "Tommy, hey, Tommy. Can you come over here?" said Mortimer.

Tommy looked up, blinked his eyes, nodded, then walked toward Mortimer and Rolando.

"Today, Tommy, today!" shouted Rolando. "Why do you move so slowly?"

Tommy stopped moving, stretched out his neck, blinked a few more times, sighed and said, "Because I'm a turtle, it's sort of expected of me."

"Have you seen Allison and Bert?" asked Mortimer.

"Yup."

"Do you know where they are?"

"Yup. They went that way," Tommy said, turned around and walked away.

"Thanks, slow poke." Said Rolando

"You're welcome." Said Tommy.

The next sign said,

Joe Broadmeadow and Levi David Walkup

Joe Broadmeadow and Levi David Walkup

(U)Ulysses the Unicorn Fish

"Hey Mortimer, How are we gonna talk to a fish?"

"I'm not sure, Rolando, but fish can see, so I bet they can hear as well. We'll just see what happens."

Mortimer and Rolando stood looking into the big glass aquarium. There were plants and rocks and then the strangest fish they'd ever seen came swimming over to look back at them.

"Will you look at that," said Rolando. "That is one weird fish."

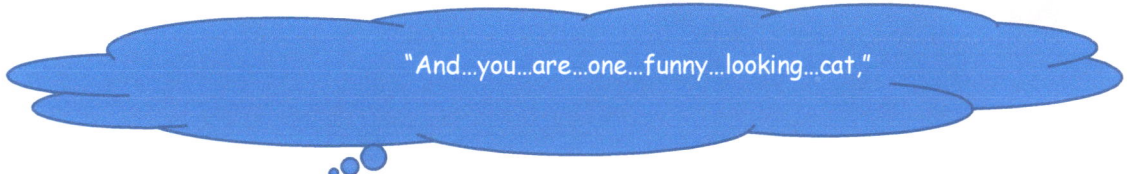

"And...you...are...one...funny...looking...cat,"

said Ulysses, the words bursting from the bubbles rising from the water.

"I AM NOT A CAT!" said Rolando. "Why does everybody think I'm a cat?"

"Well, you do sort of resemble one," said Mortimer, trying to hide his smile.

"No, I do not. I am much more handsome. Now, please Ulysses, can you tell us where Allison and Bert went?"

Ulysses turned and pointed his snout toward the next sign.

Veronica the Vampire Bat

Joe Broadmeadow and Levi David Walkup

Joe Broadmeadow and Levi David Walkup

(V) Veronica the Vampire Bat

As Mortimer and Rolando got to the entrance of the cave. Rolando stopped walking.

"I'm not going in there, it's dark and creepy."

"Come on, Rolando, bats don't like bright lights so we have to go in the cave to talk with them."

"I don't know about this," said Rolando, holding tight to Mortimer's leg. "I don't know."

Inside the cave, it took a moment for their eyes to adjust. Then movement up ahead startled them both. A second later, a vampire bat flew past then roosted, upside down, on the cave ceiling and looking down on them.

"So, I hear you're trying to find out about the alphabet and letters," said Veronica.

"How'd you hear that?" asked Rolando, clutching even tighter to Mortimer.

"Bats have excellent hearing," said Veronica. "Allison and Bert were just here. They can't be far ahead. I know they'll be happy to help."

With that, Rolando rushed from the cave followed by a much less scared Mortimer.

"See, you survived," said Mortimer

The next sign said,

Willie the Wildebeest

Joe Broadmeadow and Levi David Walkup

(W) Willie the Wildebeest

"Let me handle this one, Mortimer," Rolando said. "Excuse me, Willie. Have you seen Allison and Bert?"

Willie took a great bound and landed right next to where Rolando and Mortimer stood.

"Wow, you can really move, can't you?" said Rolando.

"Yes, us wildebeests are fast runners and jumpers. As for Allison and Bert, they are right over there." He pointed to the next sign.

Joe Broadmeadow and Levi David Walkup

Joe Broadmeadow and Levi David Walkup

(X)Xena the Xerus

Mortimer and Rolando ran to catch up to Allison and Bert. They were both concentrating on painting the new sign for the latest addition to the zoo, a Xerus.

"Excuse us," said Mortimer, "we're trying to learn about the alphabet and letters and we're hoping you can help."

Allison and Bert looked at the two curious friends.

"We'd be happy to," said Allison, "watch while we paint this sign."

With that, Bert took a brush and finished filling in the letters. X E N A   T H E   X E R U S.

"What's a X E R U S?" said Rolando.

"I am," said Xena.

They all looked as a small squirrel-like creature smiled at them.

"Wow," said Rolando, "I've never seen a Xerus before. Very cool."

"Can we follow you to the next sign?" said Mortimer to the sign painters.

"Of course," said Allison. "We are off to finish the sign for

Joe Broadmeadow and Levi David Walkup

(Y) Yogi the Yak

Mortimer and Rolando followed Allison and Bert to the next sign. They were fascinated as Allison carefully spelled out the words, Y O G I T H E Y A K while Bert filled in the colors.

"How do you know what to put on the sign?" said Rolando.

"We know the animal's name and what kind of an animal it is so all we have to do is spell it out with the right letters," said Allison.

"Letters!" shouted Mortimer and Rolando. "We've been trying to learn about letters. Where do you get the letters?"

"From the alphabet," said Bert.

"Alphabet! We've been looking for that too."

"Let's go finish the last sign and we'll show you the letters of the alphabet," said Allison. "The last sign is…"

Joe Broadmeadow and Levi David Walkup

Joe Broadmeadow and Levi David Walkup

(Z)Zina the Zebra

Zina the Zebra stood at the edge of her enclosure watching as the group of four came toward her. "Are you here to do my sign?" she said.

"Yes we are, Zina, and Rolando and Mortimer are here to watch us.

"Can they spell?" asked Zina.

"Nope," said Rolando, "but we are here to learn."

With that, Allison and Bert got to work.

Z I N A   T H E   Z E B R A.

In a few moments, the sign was done.

"Very cool," said Mortimer.

"And so simple," said Rolando.

Allison reached into her cart and pulled out a long piece of wood. "I am going to write out the alphabet for you so you can take it with you."

"That would be great," said Mortimer. "Then I can show it to Levi."

With that, Allison and Bert got to work and wrote out the whole alphabet for them.

Joe Broadmeadow and Levi David Walkup

Mortimer and Rolando thanked Allison and Bert, took their brand-new alphabet sign, and went back home to show Levi all they learned from their adventure at the zoo.

And from that day on, they always knew about every letter in the alphabet. When Levi was ready, they would teach him all he needed to know!.

About the Authors

Joe Broadmeadow retired with the rank of Captain from the East Providence, Rhode Island Police Department after twenty years. Assigned to various divisions within the department including Commander of Investigative Services, he also worked in the Organized Crime Drug Enforcement Task Force and on special assignment to the FBI Drug Task Force. Yet his imagination was always there, lurking just below the surface.

Joe is the author of numerous books; three novels based on his experiences as a police officer, Collision Course, Silenced Justice, and A Change of Hate. He has also written Saving The Last Dragon (a Y/A trilogy), and four non-fiction books.

With the arrival of Levi David, Joe has found unending inspirations for new stories and adventures.

When Joe is not writing, he is hiking or fishing (and thinking about writing). Joe completed a 2,185-mile thru-hike of the Appalachian Trail in September 2014. After completing the trail, Joe published a short story, Spirit of the Trail, available on Amazon.com in Kindle format.

Joe travels the world with his wife Susan

Levi David Walkup just recently made his appearance on this planet. While his accomplishments thus far have been limited to creating unique bubble noises and entertaining everyone with his smile and infectious laugh, his potential is unlimited.

His joyful presence is the inspiration for this book and undoubtedly many more to follow.

Levi also travels the world, expanding his horizons with each passing day. There is no doubt more will be heard from this remarkable bundle of wonder.

Levi would love for you to share this book with all your family and friends.

About JEBWizard Publishing

JEBWizard Publishing offers a hybrid approach to publishing. By taking a vested interest in the success of your book, we put our reputation on the line to create and market a quality publication. We offer a customized solution based on your individual project needs.

Our catalog of authors spans the spectrum of fiction, non-fiction, Young Adult, True Crime, Self-help, and Children's books.

Contact us for submission guidelines at

https://www.jebwizardpublishing.com

Info@jebwizardpublishing.com

Or in writing at

JEBWizard Publishing

37 Park Forest Rd.

Cranston, RI 02920

www.ingramcontent.com/pod-product-compliance
Lightning Source LLC
LaVergne TN
LVHW070408070526
838199LV00016B/537